Spiders
and other
Deadly
Animals

By James Buckley Jr.

Series Editor Deborah Lock
US Senior Editor Shannon Beatty
Senior Art Editor Ann Cannings
Producer, Pre-production Nadine King
Picture Researcher Nishwan Rasool
Senior DTP Designers Neeraj Bhatia, Jagtar Singh
Art Director Martin Wilson

Subject Consultant
Derek Harvey
Reading Consultant
Linda Gambrell, Ph.D.

First American Edition, 2016
Published in the United States by DK Publishing
345 Hudson Street, New York, New York 10014

16 17 18 19 10 9 8 7 6 5 4 3 2 1
001—285375—July/16

A catalog record for this book is available from the Library of Congress.

ISBN: 978-1-4654-5209-2 (Paperback)
ISBN: 978-1-4654-5211-5 (Hardcover)

DK books are available at special discounts when purchased in bulk for sales promotions,
premiums, fund-raising, or educational use. For details, contact:
DK Publishing Special Markets,
345 Hudson Street, New York, New York 10014
SpecialSales@dk.com.

Printed and bound in China.

The publisher would like to thank the following for their kind permission to reproduce their photographs:
(Key: a-above; b-below/bottom; c-center; f-far; l-left; r-right; t-top)
4 Alamy Images: Phil Degginger (b). **Dreamstime.com:** Aniszewski (t/background). **5 Alamy Images:** RGB
Ventures / SuperStock (b). **Dreamstime.com:** Photomyeye (t). **6-7** naturepl.com: Jurgen Freund. **9 Getty Images:**
James Tyrrell. **10 123RF.com:** Prakaymas Vitchitchalao (br). **11 Dreamstime.com:** Johncarnemolla (t). **12
Dreamstime.com:** Aniszewski (t). **13 Getty Images:** Geoff Scott-Simpson. **15 Alamy Images:** Morley Read. **16-17
Getty Images:** Snowleopard1 (t). **20 Alamy Images:** Barry Turner (c). **Corbis:** Stefan Sollfors / Science Faction
(b). **21 Getty Images:** Jernigan,Larry F (t). **24 Dreamstime.com:** Aniszewski (t/background); Danolsen (c). **Fotolia:**
Dark Vectorangel (tr). **25 Alamy Images:** Lawrence Stepanowicz (b). **Corbis:** John Giustina (t). **26 Dreamstime.
com:** Aniszewski (t). **27 Alamy Images:** imageBROKER. **28-29 Corbis:** 68 / Patrice Coppee / Ocean. **30-31
Corbis:** Demotix Live News. **32-33 Alamy Images:** age fotostock. **34-35** naturepl.com: Visuals Unlimited. **36-37
Alamy Images:** Guillermo Lopez Barrera. **38-39 Corbis:** Patrick Robert / Sygm. **40 Dreamstime.com:** Vaclav
Volrab (tr). **41 Corbis:** Piotr Naskrecki / Minden Pictures (crb). **Dorling Kindersley:** The Natural History Museum,
London (cl); Paolo Mazzei (clb). **Dreamstime.com:** Loki407 (bl); Bruce Macqueen (cr). **Getty Images:** George
Grall (cla). **42 Dreamstime.com:** Aniszewski (t). **45 Corbis:** Joe McDonald. **46-47** naturepl.com: Robert Valentic.
48 Alamy Images: Dinodia Photos (b). **Dreamstime.com:** Kristian Bell (t). **50-51 Corbis:** Jasper Doest / Minden
Pictures. **52 Getty Images:** suebg1 photography. **54 Corbis:** Pete Oxford / Minden Pictures. **56 Dreamstime.com:**
Alextara (ftl); Debra Boast (tr). **56-57 Getty Images:** Joel Sartore (c). **57 Dreamstime.com:** Alextara (tr). **58
Dreamstime.com:** Anna Kucherova (cr). **59 Dorling Kindersley:** Jerry Young (tr). **60 Dreamstime.com:** Aniszewski
(t). **61 Dreamstime.com:** Sergey Uryadnikov. **62-63 Dreamstime.com:** Paul Banton. **64-65 Dreamstime.com:**
Gvision. **66 Dreamstime.com:** Willyambradberry (t). **67 Dreamstime.com:** Rhk2222. **69 Corbis:** NIC BOTHMA /
epa. **70-71 Getty Images:** Louise Denton Photography. **74 Dreamstime.com:** Aniszewski (t). **77 Corbis:** Sylvain
Cordier / Copyright : www.biosphoto.com / Biosphoto. **79 Corbis:** Konrad Wothe / imageBROKER. **81
Dreamstime.com:** Isselee. **83 Getty Images:** David & Micha Sheldon. **84 Dreamstime.com:** Claire Fulton. **85
Corbis:** Richard du Toit. **86-87 Dreamstime.com:** Lizelled9185. **89 Dreamstime.com:** Igor Stramyk (crb)
Jacket images: *Front:* **Dorling Kindersley:** Jerry Young br, Liberty's Owl, Raptor and Reptile Centre, Hampshire,
UK cla; **Getty Images:** Remco Douma; *Back:* **Dorling Kindersley:** Weymouth Sea Life Centre tl

All other images © Dorling Kindersley
For further information see: www.dkimages.com

A WORLD OF IDEAS:
SEE ALL THERE IS TO KNOW
www.dk.com

Contents

Animals vs Humans

A woman in Tennessee felt a sharp pain in her leg. She had been bitten by a brown recluse spider! A painful rash started to spread as the spider's venom destroyed her living tissue. Thanks to quick-acting doctors, the woman survived, but had to have both of her legs **amputated.**

A man in California was on a paddleboard in the ocean when he felt something bump into his board. In just seconds, he was in a race for his life, pursued by a great white shark! He made it to shore just ahead of the snapping jaws.

In Arizona, a man was mowing his lawn when he disturbed a bees' nest. These were not ordinary bees—they were killer bees! They poured out to defend their hive. The man ran, but was stung more than 1,000 times. He barely survived.

All of these people came face to face with death from an animal, and they were the lucky ones who survived to tell their tales. That's not always the case, of course. Thousands of people die every year in encounters with animals. Tens of thousands more are injured. The people are bitten, clawed, eaten, scratched, drowned, or stabbed. Nature is sometimes not very cute or kind.

We live among animals all around the world. We're just another animal species to them, and since some animals eat other animals, this makes us potential targets for some of the larger beasts of the world. Smaller animals like spiders, snakes, and **insects** are just defending themselves. They don't care that their defense is deadly to us.

When aggressive, these weaver ants bite and spray an acid, which can blister our skin.

That's the story of the animals in this book. These are the ones that can cause greatest harm to us. In nearly every case, they are not hunting us down, but defending themselves from us. To them, we are the big, scary beasts.

Should we be afraid of animals? Afraid is not the right word. We should be cautious and careful. When we interact with the natural world, we are part of it and have to follow its rules. Don't mess with a snake, and it won't mess with you. Don't step on spiders, and they won't bite you. Don't try to sneak up on a lion to take a selfie. That won't go well at all!

In fact, animals have much more to fear from us than we do from them. For every person bitten by a spider, millions more spiders are needlessly squished underfoot. For every snakebite victim, millions more snakes are killed out of fear and sometimes for food. We are destroying animals' **habitats** and making their survival harder. So if they fight back when we get too close up, invading their home, you can't blame them. But you can try to make sure you don't become a story in this book.

Why might an insect, spider, or snake attack a human?

The Cutest Killers

In the pages ahead, you'll meet a lot of the usual killers from the animal world, such as spiders, snakes, and sharks. However, some very cute and sweet-looking animals can be deadly, too. Here are some of the cutest deadly animals in the world, explaining what makes them cute (check) and deadly (cross):

Deer

 Deer gaze out from gentle faces and their babies look so helpless! They also help spread plant seeds through their poop.

 People are killed every year when their cars run into deer darting across the road.

Slow Loris

 What's not to like? Look at those big eyes and tiny toes!

 If a slow loris licks its venom, which comes from a gland on its arm, and then bites, it can send a person into dangerous shock.

Platypus

 These are one of the few mammals that lay eggs. They also have that really cool duckbill!

 The back legs of males have sharp, venom-tipped spurs, which can cause a painful injury.

Blue-ringed Octopus

 With eye-catching beautiful skin, these octopi move in balletlike ways in their watery homes.

 This octopus has a razor-sharp beak and enough venom in one bite to kill 20 people.

Moose

 What a charmer with its cheeky grin! Their babies look so furry and cute, too.

✗ As well as causing car accidents, a moose can charge very aggressively, especially if defending its calf.

Chapter 2

Into the Web with Spiders

Spider bites are rare, but they can be deadly. One man in Australia was almost another tragic statistic:

While gathering clothes from a drying rack, an Australian man named Josh felt a sharp pain in his neck. He dropped the clothes and realized what had happened. He had been bitten by a funnel-web spider, one of the deadliest on the planet. In less than a minute, his fingers and toes were tingling. Josh began sweating a lot. His body was shutting down.

An ambulance came quickly and

rushed him to a hospital. He was nearly dead when he arrived. In fact, moments later, his heart stopped and had to be restarted with an electric shock from a defibrillator. Doctors pumped antivenom medicine into him over and over.

Thankfully, Josh was young and strong and after several days in the hospital, the medicine helped his body get rid of the venom. Now Josh warns everyone in Australia to shake out any clothes left outside!

Are you scared of spiders?

If you're scared of spiders, you're not alone! Fear of spiders is called arachnophobia and these eight-legged critters are one of the top things that scare people. However, out of more than 40,000 species of spiders in the world, only about a dozen kinds can really hurt you. Of course, the species that do have venom deadly to humans can be really, really bad!

Spiders are described as **venomous**, not poisonous. What is the difference? Venom is injected through a bite or a sting into the skin of prey; poison is ingested through the mouth or nose. Spiders use a pair of fangs to inject venom into their prey. If a spider bites a big cockroach, for instance, the venom stuns the prey, then the spider injects digestive juices, turning the insect's insides to goo. The spider then uses a mouthpart that acts like a straw to suck it all out. Gross!

Most spiders do this, but only a few have venom that can hurt a large animal like us. Spiders usually eat insects, so their venom doesn't need to be that powerful. Also, spiders are mostly very shy, so you have to surprise them to make them bite. They're just defending themselves. They don't want to eat you!

The case of the black widow

The most famous dangerous spider is the black widow. The female black widow is very dangerous to male spiders. They were given their name because many species of black widows eat the males after mating.

Black widows have dark black body parts and eight legs, like all spiders. On the female, there is an hourglass-shaped red mark. These spiders make their nests in buildings and trees. When they are in buildings, they can sometimes cross paths with people. A farmer visiting an **outhouse** where there are plenty of flies might get a bite on a certain unreachable spot, since spiders love living there among the flies.

Black widows can also sometimes be found in crates or bags of fruit, having hitched a ride from the plant. A woman in Vermont was bitten when she reached into a bag of grapes without looking. The good news is that although black widows bite about 2,000 people a year in North America, only a tiny handful of those people get very sick and deaths are very, very rare.

Even hairs can hurt!

Tarantulas look very scary! Covered with pointy hairlike bristles, with big, thick legs and bodies, they do look like a frightening spider. They have large fangs, which can inflict a painful bite. Like other spiders, though, they don't want to eat you, so if you are nice to them, they won't bite. Many people choose tarantulas when they want a spider for a pet.

More than 900 types of tarantulas live around the world. One trait they all share is hairiness. It's not really hair, which is just a trait of mammals. These **arachnids** have scratchy bristles called "urticating" hairs because they can be flicked off to bother an attacker. The bristles catch on the attacker's skin and cause great itching. Don't get them in your eyes or you could have a real problem!

The biggest tarantulas don't just eat insects but also frogs, fish, and even snakes. In Brazil, the giant bird-eating spider is almost a foot across!

Truly deadly

Most spiders can't hurt you, but some can, and do, pack a deadly bite in those rare cases that people get in their way. The Brazilian wandering spider is considered to have the most powerful venom. However, they live in the rain forest and avoid people, so bites are very rare.

The brown and red widow spiders in Australia have been the cause of some human deaths, but new antivenom drugs have helped stop that now.

Brazilian wandering spider

Brown widow spider

Brown recluse spider

Brown recluse spider bites can cause great damage to human skin and has gotten a lot of attention in the news. Fast treatment can save most people from death, however.

The funnel-web spider is probably the cause of more spiderbite injuries and death. The bad news is that they are really aggressive and often deliver several bites at once, increasing the amount of venom delivered. The good news (unless you're Australian) is that they live in far-off Australia!

Funnel-web spider

Other deadly arachnids

Spiders are not the only arachnids that can hurt people. Just like spiders, scorpions have eight legs and two main body parts, but they also sport large pinching claws, which they use to pick up prey. What sets a scorpion apart most is its large, curving tail section. This tail can whip forward to stab a prey or an attacker (or a big toe if you step near one). At the end of the tail is a stinger called a telson. It injects venom into whatever it stabs. This venom causes pain and in some cases can even kill.

The deathstalker scorpion has really earned its name. Some estimates say more than 1,000 people a year are killed by these animals. The scorpions aren't going to eat the people, of course, they're just defending themselves. Walking carefully in their habitat—including shaking out shoes left out in campgrounds—is a great way to avoid scorpions' stings. The deathstalker is also helping to save lives. Its venom has been used by scientists to help treat brain diseases, among other human illnesses.

This fattail scorpion is found in dry places in Africa and the Middle East.

The Webbies

It's awards time!

The votes are in and here are the results for categories of web-spinning!

Strongest web strands

The Darwin's bark spider was found in Madagascar in 2010. Scientists say that its web is the strongest thing made by an animal in the world!

Biggest web

Darwin's bark spider wins again! Its webs can be more than 80 ft (24 m) wide, which is large enough to cross a river!

Messiest webs

While some spiders make beautiful, geometric patterns, this black widow spider's web is a mess like a teenager's room.

Highest spider webs

In 1973, scientists brought spiders on board the space station Skylab to see if the spiders could spin webs in **zero gravity**. They could!

Most decorated webs

The yellow garden spider is one of many species that decorate their webs. These spiders add webbing in places on their webs to make additional patterns. These thicker strands form amazing patterns of their own.

Chapter 3

The Buzz on the Deadly Insects

Any human being is much bigger than the biggest insect, but put a couple of thousand insects together and you can have real trouble!

Jordan and his dad were walking their dog one evening in Florida. It was a nice night for a stroll . . . until the dog accidentally disturbed a hornets' nest. In seconds, Jordan, his dad, and the dog were under attack! Thousands of hornets poured out to defend the nest. Jordan and his dad ran, but the swarm pursued. They were stung thousands of times in just a few minutes! Even their dog was stung over and over through its thick fur.

Neighbors ran to help, and one of them was a beekeeper, so he knew how to get the insects off the pair. Still, both Jordan and his dad ended up in the hospital for many days, recovering from the attack.

We are completely outnumbered. There are billions and billions of insects on the planet with us. Most of them, thank goodness, are not out to get us. Most insects are helpful. They eat rotting flesh, decaying wood, and garbage; they eat the bad bugs; they help **pollinate** plants; they have even eaten themselves! Have you ever eaten a fried cockroach? Crunchy!

Some kinds of insects are truly dangerous to humans, though. They might be small, but they can pack a deadly punch. These are some of the tiniest and deadliest creatures in the world.

The number 1 killers

Snakes? Nope.

Fierce lions? Wrong again!

Great white sharks? Not even close.

The title of "deadliest type of animal in the world," by a long shot, belongs to one of the smallest animals on earth.

Mosquitoes are responsible for hundreds of thousands of deaths every year, and they've been acting as killing machines for centuries! It's not their sting that kills, however, it's what they bring with them.

Some species of mosquitoes carry germs that cause terrible diseases, such as malaria, yellow fever, and West Nile fever. When a mosquito stabs its sharp, beaklike mouthpart into a person's skin, it sucks out blood that it needs to live on. As it is feeding, the mosquito can pass germs into the person's blood. If a mosquito is carrying the germs, within days of being bitten, a person can be dead.

Female mosquitoes are the ones doing the biting. They need blood—from a **mammal** or a bird—to help them make eggs. They are also the silent ones, so if you hear a mosquito buzzing, it probably isn't the one to worry about!

Important note: just because you were bitten by a mosquito does not mean you will die! The mosquitoes that pass on diseases live mostly in African rain forests, in swampy areas of the Caribbean and South America, and other places you probably don't spend a lot of time. Of course, if you do live in those areas, make sure you use bug spray and sleep under a mosquito net!

Killer bees

Sometimes a good idea turns into a deadly one. In 1956, scientists in Brazil brought African honeybees to their country. They wanted to breed a new type of bee that could live in the hot weather of Brazil and other South American countries. This would help pollinate plants there so they would grow better.

Unfortunately, these bees turned out to be very aggressive and even dangerous. "Normal" honeybees do not attack a **predator** or threaten together. Instead, a few might try to sting, but most just fly away when bothered. In contrast, when bothered, the "Africanized" honeybees attack in huge swarms, delivering hundreds or even thousands of stings at once.

32

Even worse, they travel great distances. In the decades since they came to South America, these "killer" bees have slowly moved north toward Central America and the United States. More than 100 people have been killed by these swarms of bees, along with many small pets, and even large livestock, such as cattle.

Only an insect expert (called an entomologist) can tell the difference between honeybees and Africanized bees. Unfortunately, the only way for us to know if a swarm of bees is dangerous is if they attack!

It just takes one sting

Killer bees are not the only stinging insects that can kill. Wasps, hornets, yellow jackets, and even some types of ants have painful stings. In most cases, the stings just hurt. Your skin might swell up a little and turn red, but the pain soon goes away. Most people's bodies can fight off the venom that comes with the insect sting.

However, some people are **allergic** to that venom. Being allergic means that a person's body cannot process that venom. In fact, it can cause terrible symptoms and can even kill. More than two million people in America, for instance, are allergic to such stings.

If an allergic person is stung, their skin can get very red and swollen. More dangerously, their throat can swell up and prevent them from breathing. In severe cases, their blood pressure might drop dangerously, too.

A person who is not allergic can receive a couple of hundred stings without danger to their lives, but an allergic person can die from just one sting. Hundreds of people die each year when stung by an insect to which they are allergic.

Bulldog ant

Ants on the attack!

Not every stinging insect flies toward you. Stinging ants just crawl, but they do so thousands at a time! For example, do NOT mess with fire ants. These tiny, but powerful, insects build mounds in dry and dusty areas. If you see one, avoid it. If the nest or the ants are disturbed, they aggressively defend their home. Thousands and thousands of fire ants pour out to attack any aggressor. Unlike bees, they can sting many times, as well as bite with large pinching mouthparts called mandibles. People who are allergic to fire ant stings can die from being attacked. A high school football player in Texas fell on a mound during a practice and was bitten so many times that he died.

Army ants are another dangerous ground insect. They are only rarely dangerous to humans, but can cause great harm to other animals and to crops. In South America, swarms of these destructive pests can spread for miles across the landscape when they go on a "march."

In Texas, a type of insect called a rasberry crazy ant swarms in such gigantic numbers that it can take over homes. They don't really bite, they just infest. People have had computers, electrical systems, and even cars destroyed by these ants' bodies piling up inside. People use a vacuum to suck up the ants, but the critters just keep coming in the millions and millions.

A plague of locusts

Grasshoppers are cute and fun to watch bounce around on the grass. Some **species**, however, can get a little out of hand. These species, known as locusts, swarm in the tens of millions at a time. They create clouds of flying beasts all with one goal: eat whatever they can as fast as they can.

Locusts are listed as one of the terrible **plagues** in the Bible, and stories of their destructive power have been told for centuries. In the 1930s, locusts raged across the American Midwest. They would land in a field, eat everything, and then vanish over the horizon. People's farms, lives, and fortunes were ruined. The locusts don't kill people directly, but their appetite can cause great harm.

Meet Dr. Pain

Dr. Justin Schimdt is an entomologist at the University of Arizona. He wanted to find out just how painful various insect stings really were. That differs from person to person, of course, so he decided to use a single person as the scale: himself.

Over the years, he has let hundreds of different insects sting or stab him, and lived to tell the tale. He created the Schmidt Pain Index to rank which insects were the most painful. Here are the "winners," along with a few comments from Dr. Pain's chart.

Dr. Pain's Top list

Bullet ant
Dr. Schmidt says being bitten by this South American insect is "like fire-walking over flaming charcoal with a 3-inch rusty nail grinding into your heel."

Tarantula hawk
"shockingly electric"

Paper wasp

Red harvester ant
"bold and unrelenting; like a drill into your toenail."

Honeybee
(non-Africanized)

Yellow jacket

Bald-faced hornet

Bullhorn acacia ant
"like someone has fired a staple into your cheek."

Fire ant

Sweat bee

Chapter
4

Slithering with Snakes

A British snake expert was bitten by a cobra, and lived to tell the tale:

Mark O'Shea spends every day around snakes. He works closely with them at a safari park in England. He knows just how dangerous and deadly some snakes can be, so he's very careful. But sometimes . . .

Mark was feeding a 10-ft- (3-m-) long king cobra when it suddenly missed the food and bit him on the leg. Though he later called it "just a nick," it was potentially the end of his career, and his life. Cobra bites kill thousands of people each year. Being an expert, Mark knew what to do. He got help right away. He was injected with antivenom medicine. He was airlifted in a helicopter to the hospital very quickly, and survived. He forgave the snake and was soon working with cobras again!

Many of us are afraid of snakes. People hate the way snakes slither around and stick their tongues in and out. People fear the dangerous fangs and the deadly venom, and how can an animal not have legs? It's just weird!

Snakes have been living with—and causing harm to—people for thousands of years. Some ancient snake fossils were more than 50 feet (15 m) long! Try running away from that!

Not every snake is dangerous, of course. In fact, out of 3,400 species of snakes in the world, just over 10 percent are actually deadly to humans. Even so, more than 2.5 million people are bitten by venomous snakes every year, and 85,000 of them do not survive the attack.

Snakebite science

Almost all snakes have some type of teeth or small fangs. The types that use their fangs to bite and inject venom are the most deadly. Vipers are a large family of snakes that have two very sharp fangs at the front of their mouths. When they close their mouths, the fangs fold backward—unless they are biting! When a viper strikes and bites into its **prey**, special glands in its head send venom shooting through hollow fangs into the prey's body. Snakes called elapids—such as cobras or sea snakes—have fangs that don't fold up when the mouth is closed.

Each snake species has slightly different venom. Some attack the prey's nervous system, and can even stop the heart and lungs from working. Other venoms over time affect the prey's flesh. The main reason for the venom is to kill animals that the snake then eats. Of course, if the animal that the snake bites is you, then you get the venom, so watch out!

World's deadliest snakes

Believe it or not, there is much disagreement about which snake wins the world's deadliest award. The main reasons are that the snake

responsible for the bite is never identified, and also that scientists can't agree on how to choose. Is it the species of snake that kills the most people? That award goes to the saw-scaled viper. But is it the snake with the most dangerous venom? Or is it the snake whose venom kills the fastest? Here are some of the other candidates:

The inland taipan lives in the Outback of Australia. Why does it get number-one votes? Scientists measure venom by how many average-sized mice can be killed by a tiny amount of a snake's venom. In the case of this scaly dude, that number is an incredible 250,000 mice. No snake tested can do more, so imagine what that venom could do to a mere person, or even 100 people!

Eastern brown snake

The Eastern brown snake, another Australian species, can kill a person with such a tiny amount of venom that it would hardly cover the period at the end of this sentence. Russell's viper and the Gaboon viper—the world's heaviest venomous snake with the biggest fangs—are both

Russell's viper

Gaboon viper

responsible for thousands of people's deaths each year. Their venom is not as powerful as the inland taipan's, but it's really bad. Why do they kill so many? These snakes often live near people, plus they live mostly on the ground, where people can step on them accidentally. When visiting the Russell's home in southern Asia or the Gaboon's home in Central African **territory**, watch where you step!

What's that rattling sound?

One of the most famous deadly snakes in the world is also the loudest. The viper species known as rattlesnakes have a hard tail. When they shake that tail, it rattles! This sharp buzzing sound is a signal to "stay away." The rattlesnake only rattles in defense, however. When sneaking up on prey, it's as silent as any snake.

The individual pieces of the rattle are called "buttons." All rattlesnakes have a rattle and the sharp fangs of a viper, but their skin patterns vary from species to species.

Rattlesnakes, like all **reptiles**, like to bask in the sun to get warmth. As reptiles, they can only keep their bodies warm from the outside, not from the inside like mammals. Humans often encounter these dangerous snakes when walking in sunny desert areas or on forest paths. As with any dangerous snake, the best thing to do is walk away and avoid the encounter. Snakes don't want to bite you; you're much too big for them to eat!

The deadly mamba

If you get bitten by a mamba and don't get immediate treatment, you're dead. One bite can kill a person in about 15 minutes. The mamba belongs to the family of snakes called African elapids.

The black mamba takes its name from the color of the inside of its mouth. It opens that mouth wide when threatened, revealing a pitch-black cavern. Green mambas usually live in trees and are not as deadly as their black mamba cousins.

The black mamba is not only deadly, it's fast. It can move along the ground faster than any other snake in the world, so keep your distance.

Go ahead—bite me!

Would you be bitten by a snake on purpose? Not for a million dollars, right? Well, a snake expert in India says that he has been bitten time and time again, and lived to tell the tales. Vava Suresh is a professional snake hunter and **conservationist** in India, saving snakes when they stray into areas where people live. He says that he has been bitten more than 3,000 times on his rescues, and more than 300 of those were by snakes with deadly venom. He has been taken to the hospital many times and nearly died during several of those visits, but he keeps going out to find, save, and help protect the snakes he loves.

What color is the inside of the black mamba's mouth?

Underwater death

You would think that going swimming would be a good way to avoid snakes. Wrong! Many types of snakes can swim, including some of the deadliest in the world. Sea snakes and some types of kraits have venom that can kill hundreds of people with a single drop! Fortunately, they are very shy and stay away from people, saving their venom for catching tasty fish.

The water moccasin lives in swampy areas in the American South. It can bite people who are fishing or walking through its boggy areas. A strong enough bite can be enough to kill, or at least make people very sick!

The case of the spitting cobra!

Cobras are well known for the wide "hoods" they spread out from their necks when threatened. They can also rise up to have their heads reach about three feet (90 cm) from the ground. Their venom is very deadly to people and animals, and hundreds die in India and Africa after being bitten. One species of cobra, however, adds another painful touch. The spitting cobra has special holes near the tip of each fang. It can spit its venom several feet. By aiming at an attacker's eyes, the snake hopes to blind the attacker, at least temporarily, so that the cobra can make an escape.

Rampaging Reptiles

Venomous snakes are not the only reptiles that might be the last thing you see.

Gila monster

One of only two venomous lizards—the other is the Mexican beaded lizard
Size: 2 ft (60 cm) long and weighs 5 lbs (3 kg)
Deadly: its strong jaws clamp down as it bites, and then its mouth passes a venom into the victim's skin.

Komodo dragon

World's largest and scariest lizard species
Size: 11 ft (3 m) long and weighs 500 lbs (225 kg)
Deadly: with its long claws and sharp knifelike teeth, it has been blamed for several human deaths and many other injuries.

DID YOU KNOW?
An iguana stands on all four feet, takes a deep breath to appear bigger, and lowers its chinflap to warn of a strike.

Alligator snapping turtle

Size: 2 ft (60 cm) long and weighs 200 lbs (90 kg)
Deadly: its massive jaws are very strong, and one bite can easily take off fingers if poked at.

Anaconda

The world's heaviest snake
Size: up to 26 ft (8 m) long and weighs 440 lbs (200 kg)
Deadly: powerful enough to kill people, it kills its victims by wrapping its body around them and squeezing tighter and tighter, or drowning them.

American alligator

Size: 15 ft (4.5 m) long and weighs 1,000 lbs (450 kg)
Deadly: alligators are not quite as fierce as crocodiles (see chapter 5), but they have attacked people.

DID YOU KNOW?
An alligator snapping turtle has a wormlike piece on its tongue to attract prey.

How to Make a Poison Dart

As the native people of the South American rain forest have known for centuries, poison dart frogs are deadly to eat. However, those same frogs help native people find others things to eat. The people extract the poison in its skin and then dip their arrows and darts into it. These are then used to kill larger animals such as pigs, birds, and large snakes. Here's how they do it:

INGREDIENTS
One poison dart frog
One dart
One wicker basket
One pointed stick for poking

1. Collect a poison dart frog in a wicker basket.

2. Tip out and pin down the frog with a stick. This will make the frog upset and scared. It will start to ooze deadly poison onto its skin.

3. Take your dart and dip the point into the gooey stuff on the frog's back. BE CAREFUL not to get it onto your own skin!

4. Carefully use your darts to shoot a larger animal.

5. Eat that animal (and say thank you to the frog).

Trivia Time: Where do poison dart frogs get the poisons for their bodies? From the ants, mites, and other creepy crawlies that they eat!

59

Chapter 5

Death in the Ocean

Surfers ride on top of the water, braving the dangers of mighty waves and crashing surf, but lurking under the surface of the water is something much more deadly:

Surf star Mick Fanning was getting ready to take off on a big wave. He was in a contest in South Africa, trying to earn another trophy for his very full shelf. Fanning has long been one of the world's top pro surfers, and is a three-time world champion. On this day, though, he was not the biggest thing in the water.

As he began to paddle, he was

shocked to see a huge, gray fin slicing through the water toward him. As he tried to head to the beach, the huge shark lunged for Fanning's board. The Aussie surfer whacked the shark on the nose! The shark peeled off, but headed back toward Fanning as he sped for the shore. Years of life in the ocean paid off, as Fanning used his surfing skills and strength to escape, but it was nearly a deadly day in South Africa. The whole thing was caught on video, which was seen by millions of people around the world. Of course, the rest of the surfing contest was canceled! A few weeks later, when Fanning returned to the ocean for a relaxing swim, it was cut short when he spotted another shark nearby—or was it the same one?

The ocean covers 70 percent of the surface of the Earth. In its inky depths live millions and millions of creatures, big and small. The majority of the time, they won't hurt people. They're too busy finding food they like to eat or swimming to the next place to find it. However, people use the ocean, too, and when ocean predators see a person, sometimes the person just looks like their next meal.

Great white shark

The most famous and fearsome killer in the sea is the great white shark. At more than 20 feet (6 m) long and weighing more than two tons, they are enormous. They also have several rows of razor-sharp triangular teeth that can saw through just about anything.

Great whites are constantly on the move, looking for prey. They often like warm, shallow water. Of course, people swimming or surfing also like that kind of water, and in some parts of the world, they connect in deadly ways. More than 80 people have been killed by great white shark attacks since people began keeping records. Hundreds of others have been bitten or threatened.

What do people swimming or surfing look like to great white sharks from below?

Great whites don't really want to eat people. From below, however, people swimming or surfing look a lot like seals or dolphins, two of the shark's top prey animals. In most attacks on people, the great whites swoop in, take a bite to taste, and then swim away. They realize that the people are not the seals they like to eat. Sadly, that one bite can cause so much damage that human victims often bleed to death before help can arrive.

The good news is that while they are scary and terrible, attacks by great whites are very rare when compared to how many millions of people enjoy being in the ocean each year. We should watch for signs and listen to experts' news, but sharks are in more danger from people due to over-fishing and polluting the oceans than we are from them.

Other killer sharks

Great whites are not the only deadly kind of shark. Fearsome tiger sharks grin with sharp, pointed, snaggly teeth, and are one of the most aggressive species. In one famous incident, young surfer Bethany Hamilton had her left arm bitten off by a tiger shark. Bethany bravely made it to shore and has since recovered. She also returned to surfing and has become a top competitor, in addition to having an inspirational story.

Bull sharks are also killer sharks, having killed at least 30 people (though some experts think that could be a much higher total). Bull sharks live near places where freshwater enters into the ocean, and they can even survive in freshwater rather than salty sea water for a time. Attacks near rivers and streams are not uncommon. The shark also has a reputation for being a bully. The Florida Museum of Natural History says that this has been thought by many experts to be "the most dangerous shark in the world."

The hammerhead shark is not normally that deadly, but an encounter with one could be nasty. A kayaker off the coast of California actually filmed his fight with a hammerhead. While fishing, the kayaker was filming with a GoPro camera on his head. Suddenly, his kayak was bumped and attacked. He fended off the shark by poking it with his paddle over and over. The shark swam away, but then charged back again and again. After several minutes, the kayaker made it to the shore—but the shark swam in the shallows, seeming to wait for another try!

Deadly stingers

Jellyfish look like some sort of alien life-form. They don't have eyes or a face, and ooze around underwater like blobs of goo. Their body parts are almost **transparent**. They have stinging, venomous tentacles dangling beneath their wavy bodies. The tentacles have tiny sharp darts that snag and kill passing fish that jellyfish then eat.

One type of jellyfish, however, is as deadly as it is odd-looking. The stingers of the box jellyfish can cause great pain and even death to humans, who swim across their path. As many as 100 people a year, according to some counts, die from a reaction to the jellyfish venom.

The fish that can kill you when it's dead. . .

The sea creatures in this chapter have to be alive to kill you. One fish can kill you long after it has stopped breathing.

The puffer fish, or fugu, is a famous delicacy in Japan. However, if it is not prepared and cooked exactly right, its poisonous flesh can kill the person eating it. Chefs have to be specially trained to serve the meal.

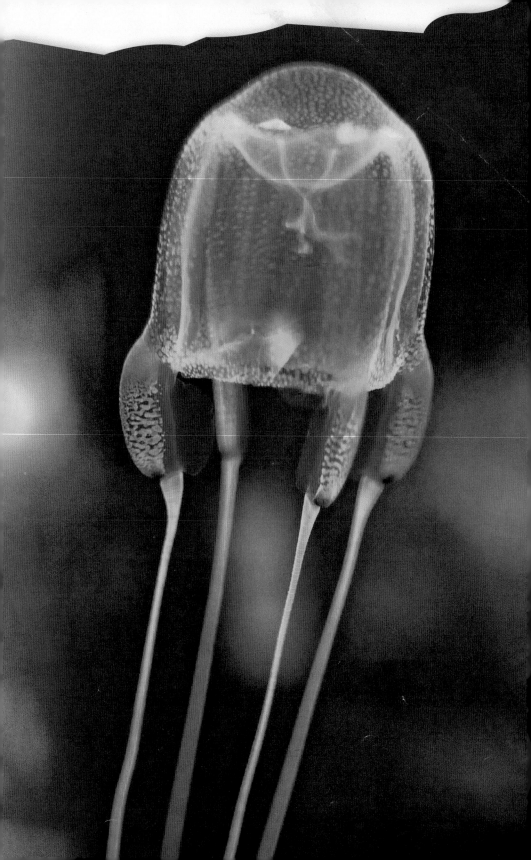

Killer crocs

Crocodiles that live mostly in freshwater in places such as Florida can be deadly. However, attacks on people by crocs in Florida are rare. Small pets are more in danger than people are. Most attacks by crocs on people happen when the people are foolish, like the golfer who tried to get his golf ball out of a pond where crocs lived. The crocs charged the golfer, and since crocs can run almost as fast as humans, he was attacked. However, be very alert along the banks of the Nile River for the Nile crocodile is responsible for the most human deaths caused by crocodiles.

In Australia, there is another species of crocodile that is really nasty to people. Saltwater crocodiles kill on average two people a year and attack hundreds more. They are very aggressive. One expert notes that a fisherman should not clean his or her catch near the water—the crocs will jump up and grab the fisherman and fish all at once! They can be 15 feet (4.5 m) long, and weigh more than 1,000 pounds (454 kg). They are fantastic swimmers, using their long tails to move through the water. They usually aim for large animals such as buffalo or boars, but they also eat large fish, including sharks. Travelers to Australia's wild northern coasts need to keep a close eye on the water, because something just might be watching them.

Ten Places to Watch Out for Fins!

Nothing quite like a day at the beach, right? Warm sun, soft sand, clear and inviting water! You lay out your towel, smear on the sunscreen, and scan the waves for fins.

❶ **New Smyrna Beach, Florida:** more than 200 attacks since 2000 have been recorded.

❷ **Brevard County, Florida:** the warm waters bring sharks and people together.

❸ **Maui, Hawaii:** surrounded by water, it's not surprising that the Hawaiian islands see shark attacks. Most are from tiger sharks.

❹ **Surf Beach, California:** attacks have happened every other year since 2008. It's a popular spot for seals, so sharks go there to find them.

❺ **Charleston, South Carolina:** the Gulf Stream brings warm water and hungry sharks.

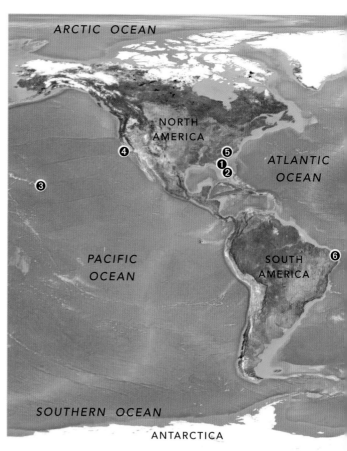

❻ **Boa Viagem, Brazil:** more than 50 attacks have been counted here recently.

❼ **Port St. Johns, South Africa:** have shark-cage tourist attractions increased attacks? There was one death each year from 2009 to 2015.

wait....! what?

If you plan on spending quality beach time at these oceanside spots, remember to wait and watch first. These are the swimming beaches around the world that most often report sightings of dangerous species of sharks.

ARCTIC OCEAN

EUROPE

ASIA

⑧

AFRICA

PACIFIC OCEAN

INDIAN OCEAN

AUSTRALIA

⑦

⑨
⑩

SOUTHERN OCEAN

ANTARCTICA

❽ **Sharm el-Sheikh, Egypt:** snorkelers need to be aware in this Red Sea resort.

❾ **Perth, Australia:** this area once had five fatal attacks in a year!

❿ **Garden Island, Australia:** a veteran diver lost an arm and a hand to a bull shark in one of several recent attacks.

73

Chapter
6

Mauled by Mammals

When we visit the woods, we are entering the home of the bears. Sometimes, they are not happy to have guests:

A man in Washington state was out for a run with his dog. The dog ran ahead and surprised a bear near the trail. The bear turned to chase the dog, and attacked the man instead. The man fought back with a large stick that he grabbed, but the bear whacked him in the head, causing a big cut. The man fell to the ground and rolled up into a ball as the bear whacked him. The bear soon became bored and left the man, who lay there bleeding—and lucky. He needed lots of stitches but he lived to tell the tale. The amazing part? This same man had been attacked by another bear four years earlier. At least, they think it was a different bear!

Bears are one of the largest and fiercest mammals that most people will ever see in the wild, but they are not the only mammals that can be deadly to people. Wolves and dogs are unafraid to attack. Like sharks, most mammals don't really want to eat people. In most attacks, the animals are defending their area or their young. In rare cases, however, people are just another animal that these top-level predators decide to show who's in charge. In nearly every case, there's not much to do but fight back or run.

Bearing up under attack

Bears are right at home in their woods. It's the humans who visit who are out of place. In nearly every story of a bear attack, the humans surprised the bear, which attacked to defend itself or its cubs. In only a few cases do the bears actually end up eating victims that they kill.

Grizzly bears are the largest and most ferocious, but black and other brown bears can be deadly, too. These are all some of the largest land mammals around. Grizzlies can top out at eight feet (2.5 m) tall and weigh more than 800 pounds (360 kg)! They have sharp claws on all four feet, along with very sharp teeth.

Since 2000, three people have been killed by grizzlies in Yellowstone Park. Of course, millions of people have visited, so the danger is still very rare. Rangers in parks all over have worked hard to educate people about the danger of bears. Campers are taught to hang their food from trees, and not keep it in their tents. Hikers are told to make noise as they walk to let bears know they are coming. Everyone knows, never get between a mama bear and her cubs!

Don't think polar bears are cute and cuddly, either. They spend most of their time far from humans, but as their world shrinks due to **global warming**, they are being seen closer and closer to towns and people. In 2011, a polar bear killed a British teenager on a hike. The young man's companion barely survived, and had polar bear teeth stuck into his skull!

In Churchill, Manitoba, Canada, it's not unusual to see polar bears walking down the streets. When that happens, everyone gets inside, quickly! Special rangers will sometimes trap visiting bears. The bears wait in "polar bear jail" (a special holding facility) before being trucked back onto the ice.

Big cats

Your house cat may act tough, but it has nothing on its oversized cousins. The big cats include lions, tigers, leopards, mountain lions, and jaguars, among others. Human encounters with these fierce beasts can cause great damage, and even death. One pair of lions was reportedly responsible for more than 35 deaths in Africa in 1898 before the pair was hunted down.

The numbers of lion attacks are hard to pin down. One count found more than 550 deaths from lion attacks since 1900; other records put the number higher, since not all attacks might be reported. The stories are easier to track. A woman on safari in 2015 was killed when a lioness leaped into the car she was in. Even "gentle" lions can be deadly. In 2013, a woman working at a lion conservation park in California was attacked and killed.

Lions are at the top of the **food chain** in the wild. Female lions are actually the more deadly gender, though males are much bigger. Lions can weigh as much as 400 pounds (180 kg). They also have very sharp claws, and powerful jaws with many teeth.

As famous as lions are, tigers actually might be the most deadly big cat. In southeast Asia, they roam around many areas where people live. The chances of crossing a tiger's path are much higher there. A study in 2013 counted up many stories and figures going back more than 200 years, and came up with a number: 373,000 people killed by tigers since 1800. However, the more recently recorded numbers are certainly going down. The main reason is that the number of tigers is plummeting. Humans have taken away so much of the tigers' habitat that the animals are critically **endangered**.

Other big cats that have attacked people include leopards and mountain lions. Mountain lions can sometimes be seen on hiking trails. Leopards are skillful climbers and stealthy nighttime hunters.

Why might there be fewer numbers of tiger attacks reported in recent years?

?

Size matters

Big, sharp claws are not the only ways that large mammals cause problems for humans. Elephants can just stomp people to death. A rampaging elephant is one you want to avoid. In India and Sri Lanka, when elephants feel like they are threatened, they will attack whatever is in their way. Sometimes, that's a whole village. Houses and buildings won't stop these powerful creatures. Some estimates say that as many as 500 people a year are killed in elephant attacks.

Cape buffalo can weigh as much as 1,500 pounds (680 kg). They are fast, too, and can charge in a group that can easily stampede over people. They also have sharp horns that can gore humans who anger them.

Hippos have been called one of the most dangerous animals in Africa. Most hippo attacks happen when the animals are defending their young. Along with being stomped upon by these 3,000-pound (1,350-kg) animals, people can be stabbed by their long, sharp teeth. Hippos also can tip over boats, causing people to drown in the hippos' watery homes.

The meanest mammal

Of course, the deadliest mammal on the planet is reading this book right now. That's right, humans kill billions more animals every year than those animals kill of us. We kill them for food, we kill to keep them from eating our plants, we squash them when they scare us, we destroy their habitats, and much more.

It's scary to think of all the animals that can really hurt humans, but it's also humbling to think about it from the animals' point of view. Consider that the next time you roll up a newspaper to whack a spider!

Who is the deadliest mammal on this planet?

Don't Forget Us!

Dear Reader,

You've just finished reading about animals from around the world that can kill you or really hurt you. But now that you're done, we're actually hurt, too.

We feel really left out, so we've taken over these final pages to make sure you know just how nasty we can be. Oh, sure, we're really pretty and have nice feathers, and we sing beautiful songs. We eat millions of insects that would otherwise bother you or your gardens, and yes, we don't have teeth.

Well, so what?! We can get very aggressive and cause a lot of damage, too, you know. OK, we're not killers like great white sharks or mosquitoes, but let us tell you, you don't want to cross some of the guys on the opposite page. Read on, if you dare!

Yours sincerely,

Birds

RAPTORS

Eagles, hawks, falcons, and other raptors have talons that can rip their victims to pieces. Sure, they almost never attack people, but if they did, it would be nasty!

CASSOWARY

Looking elegant with a long neck and super-sharp bill, it's the huge claws on their strong legs to watch out for!

OSTRICH

These guys can deliver a painful kick with their powerful legs. They're also faster than you, but thankfully unlikely to chase!

SWANS

So beautiful, so serene, so lovely—and so nasty! Swans are some of the grumpiest birds in the world. If you get near them or their nests, they will come at you with feathered fury! You'll remember getting pecked by one of these bad guys!

Deadly Animals Quiz

See if you can find the answers to these questions about what you have read.

1. How many people can be killed in one bite from the poison of a blue-ringed octopus?

2. What marking does a female black widow spider have?

3. What can a tarantula do with its urticating hairlike bristles?

4. In which country do the brown and red widow spiders live?

5. What insect holds the "deadliest type of animal in the world" title?

6. Which type of ants attack in their thousands by stinging and biting if disturbed?

7. What is a group of locusts called?

8. Which snake from the Outback in Australia has venom that can kill 250,000 mice?

9. Where does the spitting cobra aim its spit?

10. Which type of shark lives near places where freshwater enters into the ocean?

11. Which fish is still poisonous if it is not prepared exactly right?

12. In which town in Manitoba, Canada, might you see polar bears walking down the streets?

13. Which is deadlier: a male or a female lion?

14. Why are hippos called one of the most dangerous animals in Africa?

15. Which bird can kick with its powerful, long legs?

Answers on page 93.

Glossary

Allergic
The body's reaction to something, such as insect bites and stings, pollen from flowers, and food, which makes the person very unwell.

Amputated
Cutting off a body's limb.

Arachnids
A group of eight-legged animals that includes spiders, scorpions, mites, and ticks.

Conservationist
A person who helps save and protect the animals in their natural habitat.

Defibrillator
A machine that uses electricity to help make someone's heart start beating again if it stops.

Endangered
When the number of a type, or species, of animal is so low that the species could become extinct (die out).

Food chain
When energy in the form of food passes from one living thing to another.

Global warming
The rise in the Earth's temperature.

Habitat
The environment in which a living thing lives. These regions provide all the needs of the living thing for survival.

Insects
A group of six-legged animals with three body parts and most have wings.

Mammals
A group of animals including humans, that have fur or hair, are warm-blooded, and have backbones.

Outhouse
A building, such as a shed, that is built onto or near to a house. The building may be used as an outdoor toilet.

Plagues
A very large number of insects or animals covering a place and causing damage. It can also mean a fast-spreading disease.

Pollinate
Passing a flower's pollen to another flower to fertilize it, so that new seeds can form.

Predator
An animal that hunts, kills, and eats other animals.

Prey
An animal hunted, killed, and eaten by another animal.

Reptiles
A group of animals with dry, scaly skin, have backbones, and mostly lay eggs.

Species
A group of animals with the same features, which can have young together.

Territory
An area of land that belongs to an animal, and has everything that animal needs to survive.

Transparent
Light can pass through so that objects behind can be seen.

Venomous
An animal that injects venom (harmful liquid) into the skin of its prey with a bite or a sting.

Zero gravity
A feeling of weightlessness.

Answers to the Deadly Animals Quiz
1. 20 people; **2.** Red, hourglass-shaped mark; **3.** Flick them at an attacker; **4.** Australia; **5.** Mosquito; **6.** Fire ants; **7.** Swarm; **8.** Inland taipan; **9.** At an attacker's eyes; **10.** Bull sharks; **11.** Puffer fish, or fugu; **12.** Churchill; **13.** Female; **14.** They can tip over boats causing people to drown; **15.** Ostrich.

Guide for Parents

DK Readers is a four-level interactive reading adventure series for children, developing the habit of reading widely for both pleasure and information. These books have an exciting main narrative interspersed with a range of reading genres to suit your child's reading ability. Each book is designed to develop your child's reading skills, fluency, grammar awareness, and comprehension in order to build confidence and engagement when reading.

Ready for a *Reading Alone* book

YOUR CHILD SHOULD

- be able to read independently and silently for extended periods of time.
- read aloud flexibly and fluently, in expressive phrases with the listener in mind.
- be able to respond to what is being read and be able to discuss key ideas in the text.

A VALUABLE AND SHARED READING EXPERIENCE

Supporting children when they are reading proficiently can encourage them to value reading and to view reading as an interesting, purposeful, and enjoyable pastime. So here are a few tips on how to use this book with your child.

TIP 1 **Reading aloud as a learning opportunity:**

- after your child has read a part of the book, ask him/her to tell you what has happened so far.
- even though your child may be reading independently, most children at this level still enjoy having a parent read aloud. Take turns reading sections of the book, especially sections that contain dialogue that can provide practice in expressive reading.

TIP 2 **Chat at the end of each chapter:**

- encourage your child to recall specific details after each chapter.
- let your child pick out interesting words and discuss what they mean.
- talk about what each of you found most interesting or most important.
- ask the questions provided on some pages and in the quiz. These help to develop comprehension skills and awareness of the language used.
- ask if there's anything that your child would like to discover more about.

Further information can be researched in the index of other nonfiction books or on the Internet.

A FEW ADDITIONAL TIPS

- Continue to read to your child regularly to demonstrate fluency, phrasing, and expression; to find out or check information; and for sharing enjoyment.
- Encourage your child to read a range of different genres, such as newspapers, poems, review articles, and instructions.
- Provide opportunities for your child to read to a variety of eager listeners, such as a sibling or a grandparent.

Series consultant, **Dr. Linda Gambrell**, Distinguished Professor of Education at Clemson University, has served as President of the National Reading Conference, the College Reading Association, and the International Reading Association.

Index